EMA
NATI
ⓞNS

EMANATIONS

POEMS

BY PRATHNA LOR

A Buckrider Book

A Buckrider Book

Published by Buckrider Books
an imprint of Wolsak and Wynn Publishers
280 James Street North
Hamilton, ON L8R2L3
www.wolsakandwynn.ca

Editor for Buckrider Books: Paul Vermeersch | Editor: Canisia Lubrin
Copy editor: Ashley Hisson
Cover and interior design: Kilby Smith-McGregor
Author photograph: Brock Dishart
Typeset in Athelas, Krona One and Form
Printed by Coach House Printing Company, Toronto, Canada

10 9 8 7 6 5 4 3 2 1

 Canada Council Conseil des Arts  ONTARIO ARTS COUNCIL CONSEIL DES ARTS DE L'ONTARIO an Ontario government agency un organisme du gouvernement de l'Ontario for the Arts du Canada

The publisher gratefully acknowledges the support of the Ontario Arts
Council, the Canada Council for the Arts and the Government of Canada.

Library and Archives Canada Cataloguing in Publication

Title: Emanations : poems / Prathna Lor.
Names: Lor, Prathna, author.
Identifiers: Canadiana 20220159416 | ISBN 9781989496497 (softcover)
Subjects: LCGFT: Poetry.
Classification: LCC PS8623.O7 E43 2022 | DDC C811/.6—dc23

for the one who sings your name

CONTENTS

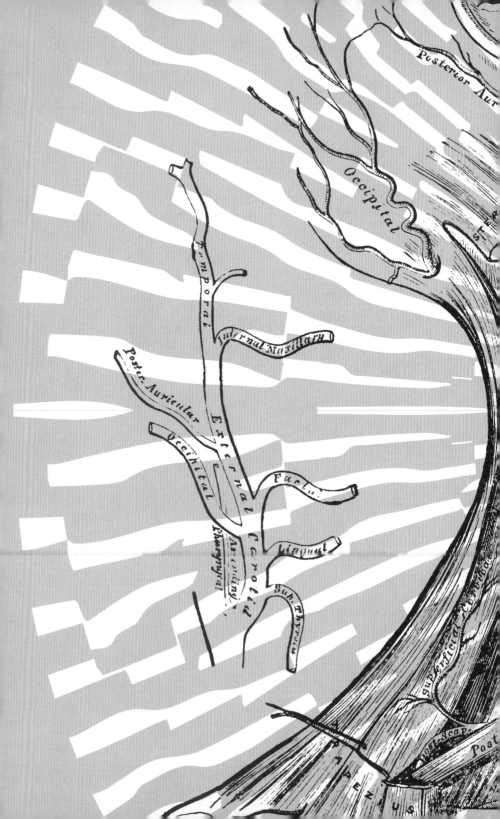

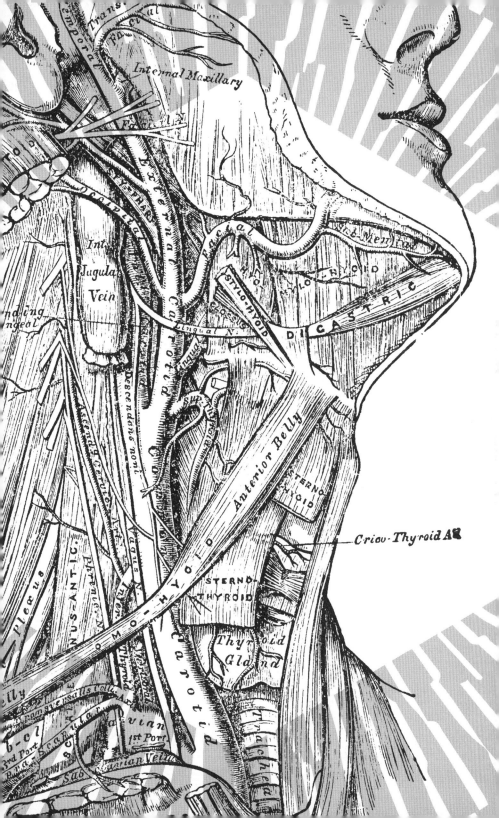

ON
SEVERAL
SERENADES FOR
BENEVOLENCE

I trot, feeling [retrospectively] like a miso-coated salmon.
– GAIL SCOTT, *SPARE PARTS PLUS TWO*

I cannot explain myself well. I coddle doubt because it protects me. I want to unspeak the history. Not because it burdens, but because it lives on the precipice. And I am there, too, on the divan, bleeding a recipe.

Near, like amber, a voice that is put away shackles itself to a figment. Tearful, futural like pools of honey: I assemble all the names I inherit and, melting, I sway from asphalt to sleep.

And now it warns your future self

How easily to slit your walk

Once you have hurled it

Severed all ligatures

And quieted the stream

The cracking face is a nearby sound

Frenzy and torpor

Turning spirit against itself

And I am a thing of human descent

You have heard

The voice

Not as betrayal

As luminescence

A slow whistle, a slip

I am naked

I thought I could write woman, and someone had already said no. But the writing of the women is.

There are so many ways you can lie beside yourself and refuse. Every day, I make amendments, but they keep me alive. I scatter my sentiments, seduce cruelty. I keep my voice low, quieting intuition.

I offer grace to everyone but myself.

Pain or murder, that is the choice – is that the choice?

Set the scene. Play it back again. We were three this time,
maybe none. I take myself out for a walk because I need
relief in the dimming world.

I am looking and someone else is, too
For a moment
I am denuded by shame that isn't mine

Pull up my legs, and then tell me something
I didn't think about what to do
I moved us along the interior of fear
I gathered my figure
And left my scent on the crossing

I want to refuse the questioning
And if I say no

In a room I am where you are not thinking.

I write endlessly in the register of prayer
Inside of my voice is our sound
Thinking the fractures
Where I emerge
From every monument
Listening for my footsteps

So, unloved – can the body ever speak?

I bare my throat

Stretching the cavity

More unlike

Piling light

Indelicate

So much goes unmissed

And so much goes

It seems simple

How the heart stops

And if I made the swan go forth

And if I made the honeydew sweat

And if I made the everyday divine

And if I stopped to call

And if the wounded were blessed

And if the belly was caressed

And if curiosity stopped

And if I could walk

How I wondered into this corridor

Swelling with delight

And no more learning

I find it unbearable to move

When you are willing

All this talking makes me drowsy

Though I long for the world

I prefer justice on the seat of my mind

I sing for duty

And acquiesce to the reign of the paragraph

culling

and adamantine

RED
BEACON

Think like a painting.

Of the dream that comes to you crawling in spoons of vermouth. Hex this last one out. In that dream, full of animosity, I bid you along to listen for the wailing.

In a cavern before a headless Buddha, heads stolen and sold, now common as decoration, where refuge was lost because the cities were emptied, because labour triumphed over thinking, over beauty. Because it was in the name of the people. I hear the serpents' call. They cloak the Buddha, shading reverie.

I follow the agony as a descendant of the viper.

Cadmium can be a beautiful word. And *I* a bang.

Dangerous thinking in a time of porousness.
Dangerous thinking in a time of possession.
Dangerous thinking in a time of prostration.
Dangerous thinking in a time of postulation.
Dangerous thinking in a time of prancing.
Dangerous thinking in a time of proclivity.
Dangerous thinking in a time of pretension.
Dangerous thinking in a time of panacea.
Dangerous thinking in a time of protrusions.
Dangerous thinking in a time of phylogenesis.
Dangerous thinking in a time of pests.
Dangerous thinking in a time of pirouettes.
Dangerous thinking in a time of panache.
Dangerous thinking in a time of the preterite.

In the archive: sensuality – no pastoral, no lyricism of the frigid, no partitioning, no moaning, no teething, no fixtures, no mist, no corollary, no ligament, no chattering, no earnestness, no dust, no cracking, no brain, no dactyls, no rancour, no frittering, no bleach, no trumpets, no high noon, no smoke, no seizures, no metres, no thievery, no remedy, no enthralling, no heroism, no draining, no berth, no settling, no tepidness, no smokiness, no machinery, no chromatics, no distillation, no force, no declining, no arcadia, no brazenness, no pleasantry, no sorcery, no anvil, no frost, no seed, no injury, no slip, no thirst, no resurrection, no method, no hollowing, no crudity, no ::

Make room for the subsonic
the little binding underneath.
What is hidden in the
substance like a sculpture
firms its place but a sculpture
can change depending on the
light the angle we perceive
how quickly we make our
approach is that

I return myself. Always
moving through

I live among the mortar
in ruin and majesty
in the tomb of prohibition

is it easier to listen
with the senses addled
discordia on the tongue
implanted fiction

is a seamless night
enough to live

I had to become fantasy
flesh as augmented
reality, excepting

there is no return
only a voice-over in a coded breach
the low hum of an invisible technology

Did you see the echo

what is left between

accident and epiphany

The joy is in me lost

and malignant

turning what gathers

carved from misgivings

I beg for another
turn in the pyre

the crossfire
of natural catastrophe
split between solid states
(were we two or were we three?)
along a feminine walk
into clairvoyance

I move between the two names
that metaphor promises me

I know faith because it touches my hand
though I have walked
across the one that matters
disappointingly

I am dented

in an unknown tense

where my breasts would be

the price of pleasure

I sold and gained stillness

so I could live

Here without wherewithal
without sanctity without
time and its history
you may anoint yourselves

among the wicked
an amphitheatre
too hushed for meaning

and sickly sweet

those furiously wild things
they call us

I prefer the dulling
and soliloquy
every mind
to the suddenness of movement

If the tempered
lacks faith

resents debt
hollows what surfaces

what presents itself as itself must always be undone

We share an alphabet
when there is movement

It makes no difference
whether the gavel is pleasant

immune
and clamouring for our recovery

the broken syllable is a cadence

unheard of

we multiply

the disturbing word

across the world

Time is direction
Time is discretion
Or time is sensing

a pulse distinct
formless

How a poem always
never lies, only
dilates what is given to speech
what is given to breath

I hear the calling
untouchable slumbering
beneath the creak

You know us by contour, darkening
the mind. I know why you came

Something exists.
I am there in a face
before I am resplendent

There is laughing and there is me
resting in an unworldly howl

I take my name because it does not belong to me
as what reflects in my fading speech

When you lick yourself
standing in the clean place
where I cannot be seen

welcome heresy
the metre
spirals into the threshold

I am beginning in the end

unbounded and vessel alike

you belong to crystal

the body obsidian

I am a woman of the disaster

seeping in the willowing

And disaster never arrives

I know my voice is

The trick is to believe everything

lives our choral signature

Each day

I return to my bed

I walk about myself

Because too much is sublime

Because I was born into doubt

I did not know my own name

I embraced the inconstancy

I won't wear the blood's

wearisome price

I am here in the present perfect
Torn out of mockery
Lies

The common measure we give up in the body
is not a question worth considering
when it is already transposed
to nearness

I welcome the calamity
between delirium
but there is a voice
in what language breaks

one incantation to another
because I may be seen
as borrowed from one time
given to another
so I appear

when tempered
reality is always disappointing

where sense must be torn

I touch my body to unknow myself

smooth the forcing

gifted as luck

living in the second person

I commit to radiance

as the coming

I make my address
unkindled

Let this be the place of my signature
since fire is already in your inventory

And there you are thinking light
an incomplete fabrication
moved by a pronoun
I am living, finally,
because I learned the death in the line

Set the scene. Play it back again. You were two – no, at least three – but they saw only one. Regardless, you lived your simulated path, locked in by demand. I am called by another name, then another. The dark follows into me, and I appear on the stream, hard and aglow.

But you know better
to not know – to float,
and live glibly.

You can dream in another tense.

The description of description itself.
Set the scene.

the wanting and the looming
the placement of the hands
the tender gap between moaning

fingering
a gutting force
they will say

it is the work
to be lilac and supple

to lie down because I have always known to trust

It does not matter if
I am flattened out
for the wanton
but not willing
to be sold as allegory
I am disorganized life
the mending
sear of reason

grasping for the breach

What if your mouth opened
before you opened it
Not as release from tenderness

But as atomic degradation
An example of our hold against fear
We will be hewn into sulphur and amnion

The music of every ancient rite
uncommitted
makes me falter
commences the stain
unshackles what will be continually lost

I am pulverized into red, and
into myself. This place makes fevered rest.
I don't know
only waywardness

Have I found "the right word" yet? Everything could be easy. I know. Someone will accuse me of my assumptions. How I move from one evil to the next. I lost the illusion. On a fantasy like tonight.

What saddens me.
What tricks me.
What moves me.
What yearns for me.
What sifts me.
What knees me.
What flirts me.
What butters me.
What irks me.
What nooses me.
What lips me.
What candies me.
What rakes me.
What ferries me.
What sits me.
What took me.
What bleached me.
What nixed me.
What primped me.
What

You can be fiction
map from one unknown to another
because the land is suspect
where I begin to know
this extended succour
the birthplace
adorns my gait
hollowing my references

I am rich with the ecstasy of a generation
though its purpose is foreclosed
in flowers and salted earth
I propel its energies because the body knows

no other path to existence

Though I have not felt the blood ripen

Or heard the trees lamenting

The shade

I see the trees and their magic

In the present perfect

The feeling is not shame

When kin massacres kin

I took the land with me as severance

"How did you know comfort?"

You built several altars and call them all home

You directed your hopes and fears toward them

And kept everything else quiet

I find myself in the slipping

Only then toward

So much of this world

Is a detour

Myself unmade

Transposed, again, in a major key

What else is heaven?

To stand and look monotonous.

I am bound because ignorance makes me sick
I am bound because ignorance makes me sick
I am bound because ignorance makes me sick
I am bound because ignorance makes me sick
I am bound because ignorance makes me sick
I am bound because ignorance makes me sick
I am bound because ignorance makes me sick
I am bound because ignorance makes me sick
I am bound because ignorance makes me sick
I am bound because ignorance makes me sick
I am bound because ignorance makes me sick
I am bound because ignorance makes me sick
I am bound because ignorance makes me sick
I am bound because ignorance makes me sick
I am bound because ignorance makes me sick
I am bound because ignorance makes me sick
I am bound because ignorance makes me sick
I am bound because ignorance makes me sick
I am bound because ignorance makes me sick
I am bound because ignorance makes me sick
I am bound because ignorance makes me sick
I am bound because ignorance makes me sick
I am bound because ignorance makes me sick
I am bound because ignorance makes me sick
I am bound because ignorance makes me sick
I am bound because ignorance makes me sick
I am bound because ignorance makes me sick
I am bound because ignorance makes me sick
I am bound because ignorance makes me sick

Rusts me into corners.

PEDAGOGY OF RIDICULOUSNESS

Obliviousness is no ignorance, who joins ridicule, sultry stature. If whatever can be said is eruption, let me speak plainly. To tell you the truth, to tell you that it won't be fair, why not embellish the already lie, and mark one's thinness with the look of hardened salt.

A cavity of delusion, rusted and splintering the tongue.

When you move do I think as a thin wet line.

Judgment out

sings the voice when it is over in its sleep

For once let's not forget the undivine

What marks me myth you've long forgotten

Is it still possible to see in such singing?

Yes, the joy transplants

When we speak

Holds love and I want to be wrong

Though I learn about this form

It is no excuse for injury

Help me beauty

Without the contour

But I want

With a fragrance

To do well against itself

For the flesh is a residue

Bends bone into service

They say many things about the body

Once it has exited

The room or returns

Unoccupied by thinking

An altar can be a place in time

If you know the reeling figure

The placement of the hands

Loosening the body

When you've hardened it

Remember you belong to crystal

For the last demand

I envy malice

I wanted freedom to mean

Like moving

So much moving

Set the scene. Play it back again.

I always keep one knee bent
to prepare for running.

I never emerge
seeking only insurgence
a moment of recovery
to listen extraordinarily.

How often do I speak to you
In a voice of what you call God or wonderments
What will it take for you to know that it's enough
To wander into marvels